PROTECTING
YOUR LAW FIRM'S
HIDDEN TREASURES:
INTELLECTUAL PROPERTY
ASSETS YOU DIDN'T
KNOW EXISTED!

Protecting Your Law Firm's Hidden Treasures: Intellectual Property Assets You Didn't Know Existed!

J.D. Houvener, Esq., MBA, PE

Sponsor: Bold IP, PLLC - 800-849-1913 - www.boldip.com

ISBN: 1546977228
ISBN 13: 9781546977223

TABLE OF CONTENTS

Chapter 1

INTRODUCTION

Every well managed business takes thoughtful and thorough steps to protect its IP, and so should every well managed law firm.

When you take stock of the multiple assets of a law firm, intellectual property is often overlooked. There is a widespread perception that law firms are different from other types of businesses because they are professional institutions of service.

This belief is perfectly understandable and acceptable. But what's not acceptable for the firm that values the protection of its IP is to assume this "professional institution of service" perception somehow provides blanket protection. It does not allow the firm to adhere to a different set of rules.

The law firm is a revenue-generating, for-profit business. Just like Google, Amazon, Facebook or Apple, the law firm sells services to its clients.

The way that the firm delivers customer service is through the level of quality of its legal services. How intellectual property factors into this is largely determined by the brand the law firm represents. This holds true whether we're dealing with a solo entrepreneur, a solo practice, a solo law firm, or a major firm with multiple partners and multiple offices. Each represents a certain level of service to potential and current clients.

The brand represents this promise, the relationship, and what the firm is expected to deliver to their customers. When the public looks at the firm's website, its advertising, or marketing materials, an expectation is created. The way this expectation is shaped, and everything that goes into shaping it, can be considered elements or ingredients of the brand.

Let's say people interested in Jane Doe's law firm, which handles criminal litigation, visit her website and read blogs. These blogs, and everything else on the site, is intellectual property the firm uses to communicate and build its brand.

We are dealing with two considerations.

1. The law firm is a business.
2. The brand, the reputation, and other intellectual property such as copyrights, patents and trade secrets, are as germane to a professional services firm as they are to any other business.

In terms of its marketing, the law firm is typically "outward facing" to the client and the prospective client. This is done to convey the firm's services and to differentiate itself from the competition.

This outward facing position benefits the prospective client. People are better informed and better able to make an appropriate decision on representation.

The law firm, which performs as a business, markets, advertises, and informs its core client base. It not only educates the prospective client, but also positions itself in the proper category. Jane Doe's criminal law practice would not be able to regularly attract new clients if it did not market itself. Without thoughtful marketing, the firm could find itself on a list of estate-planning attorneys, clearly a waste.

❖ ❖ ❖

THE CREATION OF ARTISTIC WORKS

Along with the actual marketing strategy, other aspects of intellectual property come into play along with brand building. A key consideration is the creation of artistic works.

How does a law firm, and how do the individual attorneys within the firm, protect their intellectual property creations? These creations can cover writings, artistic works, or even the performing arts. Performing arts cover an attorney in front of a camera, or in front of a microphone recording audio for podcasts, webcasts, or any pre-recorded media.

In the pages ahead, we'll look at this and we'll also briefly examine patent law. Patent law can be as applicable to a law firm as with virtually any other technology company.

A law firm may be innovative in multiple arenas:

- Computer science
- Software development
- Novel methods for marketing
- Innovative processes for handling clients' cases
- Client relationship management software

Much like any other business, the firm's trade secrets are the secret sauce. They help determine how the firm positions itself and competes. Law firms utilize confidential processes, keep confidential client lists, and maintain proprietary lead sources.

There's a lot of ground to cover and a lot to protect.

Given the breadth and depth of trade secrets and intellectual property, a prudent starting point for the process is insuring proper protection for the firm's brand.

NOTES

Chapter 2

THE BRAND OF A LAW FIRM

Law firms should consider how best to define and build their brand, and then, how to nurture and safeguard the brand once it has been established.

The brand of your firm may be built on the names of its partners, or in the case of a solo practice, on your name.

But the elements of the brand can easily venture far beyond a name, and embrace everything from colors used in communication materials to the actual feelings and emotions the brand evokes.

The brand represents the source identification for goods or services. If your firm is like most, you believe you deliver professional services rather than physical goods.

But this distinction bears examination. It is the distinction between the tangible and the intangible.

In many ways, your firm does market and provide goods. One of the most common goods is created through software.

Quite often we see that law firms, especially those in litigation, undergo an extensive amount of discovery using software to record and manage information.

An associate, or someone performing the research and information gathering, may be using proprietary software tools to identify germane keywords, phrases, or legal definitions. A special process is used to source whatever the parties are looking for in the documents.

The findings are then organized, and subsequently presented to partner level attorneys at the firm to present to the court.

The software used in this process may be sold to other law firms, or it could be sold to clients for use in their own companies where in-house attorneys are on staff.

This software is one example of a good. It is a physical product. It is clearly IP that warrants protection because there is demonstrable commercial value.

In the overall context of how the firm currently generates revenue, this software may be relatively insignificant. But its impact could easily change. Today's relative financial insignificance should not justify the absence of protection.

❖   ❖   ❖

SERVICE

The predominant means of commerce for a law firm is clearly service. It is the process of providing counsel, legal advice, and representation in front of an opposition, whether it be at a proceeding or before a government body.

These capabilities and this provision of a professional service bring us back to the firm's brand, which can include anything that falls under The Lanham Act.

❖   ❖   ❖

The Lanham Act is America's federal trademark statute of law. It prohibits trademark infringement, trademark dilution, and false advertising.

Enacted in 1946, key aspects of the act are the trademark registers. There are two subchapters which address this.

Subchapter I provides the requirements that a mark must meet to receive a registration on the Principal Register. It grants rights to the trademark owner to prevent others from infringing their mark.

Subchapter II defines the form of registration on the Supplemental Register, for certain marks that are do not qualify for registration under Subchapter I, but may be registrable in the future. Many of these marks are descriptive. This form of registration lacks the degree of protection of Subchapter I.

(Pub.L. 79–489, 60 Stat. 427, enacted July 5, 1946, codified at 15 U.S.C. § 1051 et seq. (15 U.S.C. ch. 22))

❖ ❖ ❖

In most instances, the firm's brand qualifies for protection under common law and under registration for trademark. Key provisions include the fact the brand name is distinctive, apart and away from the service that is being rendered.

❖ ❖ ❖

CREATING THE APPROPRIATE DISTINCTION

A distinction must demonstrate that the name of the law firm itself cannot be merely descriptive.

For example, a divorce attorney in Seattle will not be able to register a trademark for "Seattle Divorce Attorneys." This is because it identifies the geography and precisely what area of law services are provided. If what's sought is to protect the brand name, it must have significance, and it must be distinguished from the actual service.

If the name of the firm is "Fresh Start" and the actual service is a divorce firm, all Fresh Start attorneys could potentially be something that could be trademarked and registered.

There are two different avenues for securing trademark rights.

The first is through establishing a business under the legal name "Fresh Start Attorneys." By doing business within the firm's home state, or even out of state, protection is provided for the geographic area of business.

Most attorneys are now working on the internet and by phone, so a growing number of clients may be out of state. The reach of service is quite broad, so over time, clients, potential clients, and others, get to know the law firm as "Fresh Start." This is the process through which a brand is developed.

Based on when that name was first used in commerce, another firm using the name "Fresh Start would not be able to use that name in competition in the same geographic market as the initial "Fresh Start" law firm.

If that initial "Fresh Start" law firm wants to conduct business in all fifty states, it would be best served to register its mark at the USPTO Trademark Office. This would safeguard the firm and help to preclude any possible future confusion regarding infringing uses. This falls under the process of registering a trademark, which we'll examine in the next chapter.

❖　❖　❖

EXTERNAL CONSIDERATIONS: THE ROLE OF THE CLIENT PERSPECTIVE

One important element of the brand deals with how the client feels about your firm, and how the client talks about your firm, when they're not speaking directly with you.

When the client talks with their friends or family, someone may ask them, "Who are you working with? Who's helping you with this issue?"

If your law firm is mentioned in their response, the way that they respond to the question is significant. Positive images, feelings, and perceptions expressed by the client represent the goal for developing the brand. Collectively, these define the foundation of how you would like the firm to be perceived.

The client's perspective of a law firm is most likely one that is professional in nature, not necessarily akin to a more traditional business.

This distinction supports the fact that any kind of marketing, sales, or presentation that creates a fresh look for a law firm will help the firm differentiate itself and stand out from competitors. The ability of the firm to execute this is key.

❖   ❖   ❖

INTERNATIONAL CONSIDERATIONS

Similar to the ways firms work with clients in other states, we see firms work with clients in other countries.

If your law firm eventually develops international reach, provides consultation, or has a physical presence in foreign countries, this justifies the need to secure international trademark rights.

When the firm conducts business in multiple countries, it should submit an application for trademark registration through the Madrid Protocol.   When only one country is involved, the application is submitted to the World Intellectual Property Organization.

❖   ❖   ❖

THE ONGOING PROCESS OF BUILDING AND PROTECTING THE BRAND

This strategic approach to protecting the brand can make a significant difference when it comes to valuing a company upon merger, sale, or acquisition of a law firm.

The brand of the firm is an asset that can easily accrue value over time. It may contribute towards the valuation of the firm in a possible future sale or merger, and drive a successful exit strategy.

Because this strategy is more thoroughly safeguarded, protections can extend beyond the state line, and beyond the borders of the United States, when international protection for the brand is granted.

Notes

Chapter 3

❖ ❖ ❖

PROTECTING THE LAW FIRM'S BRAND

When you file a trademark application as a law firm that will conduct business within one state only, you only need to apply for your own state's trademark registration.

If you'll conduct business outside the state, or believe you may eventually do so, it is prudent to register with the United States Patent and Trademark Office.

There are two options for this.

❖ ❖ ❖

REGISTRATION OPTION 1

If you're already in business, and selling and conducting business and service using the name or logo you're seeking registration for, you can file the registration. When you file, you will need to show an example. This is known as a specimen of use, and it can be as simple as providing a sales receipt with an out of state client.

This is the type of specimen the Trademark Office requires as evidence that you are providing service outside the state under the name or logo you are trademarking.

❖ ❖ ❖

REGISTRATION OPTION 2

If you are launching your firm and because you're new, you can't demonstrate actual use of the brand you plan to build, you can file what's known as an Intent-to-Use application.

This application attempts to reserve the requested name and/or logo. The word, mark, or the logo can be filed and you can seek to conduct business at some point within the next 18 months.

Once the application is submitted, you have formalized intent to use that name in commerce for that legal services that you're providing. The evidence and that specimen of use, the sales receipt, online commerce activity, or commercial activity, will need to be demonstrated to the Trademark Office within an 18-month window. In some situations, this time frame may be extended.

❖ ❖ ❖

ENFORCING YOUR TRADEMARK

Once a brand of the firm is protected and registered with the Trademark Office, enforcement mechanisms are the same as any other business.

In the event another firm infringes on your brand, the traditional cease and desist letter puts the infringing firm on notice. There could be multiple reasons for the infringement, ranging from the date of the other firm's trademark registration to the geographic limits of protection.

The goal of the cease and desist letter should not be to intimidate. The letter should be thoughtfully prepared with sufficient facts to help the infringing firm grasp the situation, so that resolution is arrived at quickly and amicably.

Demonstrating your own firm's commercial use is essential. So is demonstrating the specific infringement, such as an actual published document.

Referencing statutes within the Lanham Act can substantiate your claims and insure that each element of the case is met.

At a high level, the letter should demonstrate that there is actual commercial use of a confusingly similar word mark, or design mark, from the one that has already been previously registered, and for which there is a prior use in commerce.

This is the standard. It is no different for the law firm than for any other business, or any other trademark enforcement mechanism. Between two law firms the only subtlety may be that the party receiving the letter will be knowledgeable about what a cease and desist letter is.

In some situations, it may be helpful for the firm which has been infringed upon to retain the services of an intellectual property firm to help represent it in the matter, particularly if the issue is significant.

At times, lawyers do need lawyers. Law firms may require counsel to make sure their interests are properly represented, and that their innovations and their intellectual property is properly protected.

A lawsuit is not the desired outcome, but in the face of an unaddressed offense, it may the only option. While this is not the best result, enforcing a trademark is essential and a step that must be taken to protect the asset and avoid public confusion.

❖   ❖   ❖

LOGOS VS. WORD MARKS

When a law firm builds a brand, it can create a graphic logo, a word mark, or a combination of the two.

Traditionally, law firms have been named after the surnames of the founders. But when it comes to building a brand for a law firm, this may not be the case. There may be a symbol or a unique distinction that the firm intends the customer to associate with the firm.

For example, a firm may brand itself and do business as "Eagle Tax Advice." "Eagle" is the distinctive characteristic. "Tax advice" is the exact service, which in general terms is not considered distinctive.

What's important about "Eagle" is what thoughts the prospective client associates with the word.

Quite often, a graphic logo is required, to solidify in the client's mind, and to frame what they receive from the attorney. This symbol can help the client think, when they see the symbol of the eagle, "That's my attorney. That's where I go to get tax advice."

It's important for the law firm to develop not only the brand, Eagle Tax Advice, but to support the brand by creating a logo or an image. This graphic element may or may not have color. What it does have is the ability to help a prospective client associate with a firm's brand. It provides a way for the firm to distinguish itself from other brands, even from brands that are not in the legal profession.

Developing the logo may be more time-intensive than developing the word mark.

As far as the trademark office is concerned, registration of a brand is separate. A design mark, commonly known as a logo, is a separate application and a separate registration from the word mark.

Many brands will combine these two. For example, in the image of the eagle the letters E-A-G-L-E, eagle, and perhaps even law, are embedded into this hybrid word and image mark.

These may be available for registration. They would be considered a design mark. Because there are images that look like letters, it is purely the design of the mark that's being protected.

It would be prudent for any business, including a law firm, to first protect the word mark that covers its brand. After this has been achieved, and the business is engaged in commerce, it can decide upon a logo that reflects its brand. This is the logo the firm should use long-term.

❖   ❖   ❖

MERGER & PARTNERSHIP CONSIDERATIONS

Protecting the law firm's trademarks may go beyond the actual firm and the brand identity, by insuring that the brand is acknowledged and remains congruent as the firm evolves and grows.

There are unique growth patterns that law firms follow. As they begin to grow, most firms tend to delegate and expand authority from a solo partner to potentially one or more partners.

As the firm brings on partners from the outside, either from other firms or from their solo practice, it is helpful for the firm to consider a prospective new partner's contributions. These contributions should be weighed not only in the context of individual performance, but in terms of how this person will embody and represent the brand of the entire firm.

There may be situations where the firm's brand needs to be adjusted and shifted to accurately and beneficially reflect the admission of a new partner.

Specific steps can be taken to identify and assess what possible brand changes should be undertaken when onboarding a new partner. A similar scenario is presented when a merger or acquisition takes place. The size of the acquired firm relative to the firm acquiring it bears consideration.

A simple process for this is to identify the business, the actual service offering the attorney was previously providing to the public. Determine how much in line this is with your law firm. Was the attorney and/or the attorney's firm offering any other services above and beyond what your law firm offers? If so, those additional practice areas should be explained to the partner's client. The client should understand those are not capabilities your firm offers.

Let's say your law firm focuses purely on family law. You bring a partner in to join your family law practice. That partner has clients who depend on him for estate planning, along with tax planning and taxation counsel. Those clients may assume that because their attorney is now with your firm that the firm will be able to address tax and estate matters.

That will not be the case given the firm's family law specialty. This is where the brand once again needs to be considered. It becomes part of the duty of the onboarding partner to inform their previous clients that representation can no longer be provided on non-family law matters.

The integrity of the brand is impacted by the incoming partner's ability to communicate this change. The need to maintain a positive perception of the brand requires this communication. As you would expect, this can easily take on even greater importance when acquiring a law firm.

Another issue that bears examination is an understanding of what publications are the property of the single attorney or the firm being acquired.

This understanding should not only include the attorney's online presence. It should expand to take in a broader footprint including the attorney's public image, publications such as court documents, blogs, social media, written opinions, articles, and, if appropriate, news coverage.

There may be situations where the individual has committed indiscretions, or has misrepresented personal achievements which may have been published. These issues should be identified and addressed to prevent or minimize unforeseen damage to your law firm's brand.

❖ ❖ ❖

THE WORK ITSELF

The obvious is often easily overlooked. The work product of the attorney is reflected in the brand. This is the actual substance of the legal practice. It is important to know precisely what the attorney or firm is producing.

As a requirement for coming on board, the attorney should deliver work that supports the existing public perception of the law firm. The actual legal work product should be evaluated to make sure it upholds these standards, accurately represents the brand, and reflects the quality of the expanded firm it will play a role in representing.

The public perception, the current client perception, and the work product are each vitally important when it comes to evaluating and onboarding a third-party individual (or subsidiary law firm) that will be merged into your firm.

These are important issues independent of financial considerations, which are driven by the desire to grow the firm and increase revenues and profitability. When decisions on an acquisition, a merger, or taking on a new partner are limited to financial considerations, the brand of the firm may be put at risk. Short-term gain may be offset by long-term erosion of the value of the brand.

It is better to base the decision on a broader set of criteria which include careful consideration of the law firm's brand and identity, and particularly, how these are perceived both by the public and by current clients.

❖   ❖   ❖

LONG TERM TRADEMARK PLANNING

When you think about a brand for a law firm, it's best to think big.

As with any business that's in the small, fledgling stage, a skilled trademark attorney will encourage the entrepreneur to look five to ten years down the road. This process will include consideration of the firm's business plan, so the trademark attorney can work effectively with the business owner to help decide what future areas of commerce the firm may wish to pursue.

This includes not only specific areas of commerce, but potentially what business entities may be involved.

If it is successful over time, a company may merge and decide to acquire additional companies. A similar situation holds true for the law practice. While a law firm may start out in patent law, it may grow and evolve into a trademark law firm because of the legal synergies that apply to both patents and trademarks. In the future, the firm may wish to handle copyright and then eventually the entire commercial property suite. Beyond this, it may wish to handle litigation for commercial properties it has helped clients acquire.

As the practice areas grow, the coverage of the brand needs to grow accordingly. A knowledgeable trademark attorney will identify those opportunities at the outset, and will help the law firm decide to what degree it should state use in commerce. Leaving these specific practice areas as legal services may be too broad, but by being specific, the firm may capture a less distinctive market.

NOTES

Chapter 4

Artistic Creations Born in a Law Firm

A creation can certainly be an oil painting, a movie, or a book. But it is also eligible for the protection of a copyright, and the process of creating a work, and the process of copyrighting a work go hand in hand.

Sometimes, many hands are involved in creating a work. We see this when multiple firms collaborate on a large project.

❖ ❖ ❖

INTERNAL CREATIONS

One aspect of protecting internal written material is specific to non-legal substance. This deals with the commercial elements of legal services, and may cover creations such as price sheets and sales strategies.

Material published and intended for internal use is typically restricted to the law firm's employees, including the management or partner levels. Examples include a written price sheet, price structures, policies, and procedures indicating when to present certain offers.

There may be documents with instructions on how to secure agreements with new clients who are brought on, and provide details on the sales process that should be followed. Clients are sold a certain level of service, and the law firm, much like any other business, will likely have documentation that outlines the process.

This information will guide the firm's employees who deliver presentations and interface with clients or prospective clients. These price sheets can be complicated and often reflect considerable thought. They may, for example, examine the issues to be considered before offering prospective clients a fixed fee for service or an hourly rate.

Whatever the specifics may be, the law firm's rate structure is likely evolving, and we are seeing a growing number of pricing innovations that warrant protection.

Hourly rates should be based on the type of work that's being requested, and consider the anticipated complexities of the work. The ability to assess and categorize the complexity based on an initial consultation or two with a potential client is a process that can qualify for protection. Written materials to guide the member of the firm meeting with the client on how to make an actual offer and present the attorney's fees may fall under this umbrella.

In a similar vein...

- There may be a process used to determine if a payment plan is an option, and if so, how it should be based on an established set of criteria.
- The firm's fee may be adjusted based on the prospective client's willingness to pay upfront, or pay over a specified period of time.
- Policies regarding payment with a debit card or a credit card.
- Policies concerning the actual processing of payments that are specific to the firm, which may address issues such as the acceptance of checks and procedures with a bank account transfer.

Each one of these internal documents should be protected. They can be protected if they were published through corporate law. If they are published under the domain of copyright law, most may qualify as trade secrets, a topic we'll address in Chapter 5.

Many law firms have created a written policy covering structure and guidance on setting fees. This information may appear in the presentation and sales format as well as in internal documents. This scenario may hold particularly true for firms using flat rate structures, that need to develop an accurate estimation of a flat rate.

The days of billing hourly and launching an engagement by securing a deposit from the client are slowly fading away. Clients are becoming less inclined to engage with a firm that is strictly hourly based. They are more educated. Clients want to know what to expect for what they pay. They want to be informed, and they don't want to be surprised.

These changes in the marketplace put growing pressure on the firm to create effective pricing policies. Given that these policies can impact the financial performance of the firm, they need to be properly protected.

❖   ❖   ❖

THE ISSUE OF "FIXED IN TANGIBLE MEANS"

There cannot be a copyright for any of the firm's creations, whether audio, visual, written, or performed, as we discussed, unless they've been fixed in tangible means.

Ideas don't qualify for protection. Documents do. Tangible means calls for something we can see, touch, and feel. It can be on paper, an audio recording, video, anything that allows ideas to be preserved and distributed.

Whoever owns the copyright enjoys the rights to control how the content is used, which covers everything from distribution to reproduction.

As soon as the content is fixed, copyright privilege can be granted. From this point, it does not matter where these documents are physically housed, because copyright protection has been granted.

This protection cannot take place without the demonstration of content being fixed in tangible means.

❖　❖　❖

LICENSING OR SELLING CREATIVE WORKS BORN IN A FIRM

In most instances, law firms underestimate the value of their creations and miss the opportunity to market them to other practices. There is often an opportunity to monetize that is not leveraged. For example, a well written schematic about estate planning that includes distinctive diagrams, flow charts, colors, and other original content, is marketable.

The firm which has secured a copyright for this creation can seek additional registration upon completion. This allows for creative expressions to be licensed or sold to third parties.

The third party can come in different shapes and sizes. It may be a departing partner or associate who wants to take the intellectual property and the creations that either they have created with the firm, or that the firm has compiled and taught over time, to use in a new venture. The intent is that the asset will be used for commercial gain, potentially by a competitor of the firm which created the intellectual property.

The law firm should have sufficient protections for its creation in place to allow for financial compensation through licensing, subscription, sale, or some other mechanism.

When an employee creates this kind of work, it automatically belongs to the law firm. It is up to the firm, its ownership and the partners, to decide the extent to which the asset will be valued. There are professional evaluation companies that can help in this process. Typically, a CPA can recommend an evaluation firm, or provide guidance on asset valuation.

❖   ❖   ❖

THE MECHANICS OF MONETIZATION

A traditional structure for monetizing the firm's intellectual property would involve some type of licensing. Because the creation delivers value to the originating law firm, the firm will want to continue using it.

An outright sale may not include licensing. This means that the firm surrenders the asset to a third party and may no longer be able to use its own expression, either for its own content or commercial use.

Putting these agreements in place correctly becomes critical. Licensing agreements for intellectual property should address both the different rights and the bundle of rights that each creative expression holds.

As an example, if there is an existing underlying copyright, the bundle at least consists of the right to make copies of, distribute, reproduce, or make derivative works.

There may be additional rights, but these represent the core of the bundle. One or more of those rights in part, meaning either a non-exclusive or exclusive deal for each of those rights can be licensed and should be considered when looking to value the license fee or outright sale.

If the firm is going to be sharing this sort of creation, both parties should consider the ramifications. There may be restrictions or protections. If the intellectual property involves marketing, specific geographic restrictions may need to be put in place to protect both the originating firm and possible additional licensees. If the creation is software code, improvements or changes to the code may need to be restricted or otherwise addressed in advance.

There are significant considerations that go beyond the scope of this discussion. The subtleties of an IP licensing agreement are numerous. The point is to be aware of the implications, to have an agreement in place, and to revisit the agreement as both technology and the actual content, the creative expression, evolve over time.

❖　❖　❖

THE FIRM'S TEMPLATES

Inside virtually every law firm, there are creations that the attorneys, staff, and paralegals create on an ongoing basis. Each one, in its own way, delivers value to the client.

Drawing on knowledge, innovation, and information flow, many of these creations take the form of internal templates. These are typically documents created in Microsoft Word templates that capture the essence of content that will be presented to the client.

This content may be put in language applicable to a variety of circumstances. The actual wording of the template allows language to be manipulated, changed, modified, and turned into a final document for client delivery without the need to generate an entirely new document from scratch.

These templates are creations. They often change over time as they evolve with changes in the law. They may also reflect necessary nuances that allow for enhanced communication or interaction. This enhanced interaction can take place between the client and the attorney, between attorney and attorney, or between attorney and partner or manager.

Whatever parties are involved, the adjustments and enhancements add value to the templates. The intellectual property becomes more valuable as the firm grows. These are essential documents that warrant safeguarding not only as trade secrets, but to include copyright provisions for ongoing protection.

If there is ever a need to publish the templates, distribute them, or to weigh their value in the event of potentially franchising the law firm, this intellectual property should be registered to the Library of Congress. Without these protections, this is work that could be legally copied and distributed without your firm's permission.

❖ ❖ ❖

THE FIRM'S WEBSITE

The website should be thoroughly protected. Blogs, descriptions of services, and other content are creative works.

❖ ❖ ❖

THE FIRM'S SOFTWARE

Software represents a major area of creation as a growing number of firms become increasingly virtual. As firms working at a distance from clients and professional associates rely on cloud networking, video conferencing, phone conferencing, software and tools that connect teams are become essential. If custom software is created within the firm, it becomes intellectual property of the law firm. It should be protected and nurtured as a creation.

❖   ❖   ❖

MULTI-FIRM ARTISTIC CREATIONS

Many cases grow over the course of weeks and months. It is not unusual for a personal injury attorney to work alongside an estate planning attorney to make sure the complete interest of the client is fully addressed.

On these projects, extensive work product is shared. When it comes to generating the type of work product that could be carried forward into new projects, there are vehicles such as templates, processes, and even the synergies between the two firms.

All of this is intellectual property. Each element should be protected and considered to be a coveted item to be kept within the collaborating firms.

This type of intellectual property typically begins with trade secrets. This is because the type of information, processes, systems, and templates can immediately become valuable to a competitor.

What if these trade secrets were to be published? What if the firm which created this intellectual property shared it with a collaborating firm, and then discovered the collaborating firm had published it, or used some of the content to create a new document such as a white paper?

Proper protection at the outset safeguards the firm from this type of activity.

Here is another scenario where the protection of intellectual property may be overlooked.

Your firm does not forgo the creation of intellectual property when it discloses to one or more law firms, or one or more attorneys, outside your own practice. Protections for this type of common law generation can be covered within the terms of the contract between the two firms, or through the engagement letter with the client.

The key point is to insure that intellectual property generated in the representation is to be owned by and not to be disseminated by the respective parties. It is to be held in confidence by the parties exchanging services.

❖ ❖ ❖

OUTSIDE LAW FIRM ARTISTIC CREATIONS

Along with documents created in a law firm on a day-to-day basis, there are also creations originated outside the law firm that should be protected, and considered part of the firm's assets. These are usually non-written works such as performances, presentations, or seminars, where the content exists in the form of audio or video.

As an example, one of your associates might give a presentation at a continuing legal education function, also known as a CLE, perhaps for the local county bar association.

Let's examine a scenario where the associate makes an oral presentation and along with the oral presentation there is documentation for the PowerPoint slides, or whatever platform is providing the visual element.

The bulk of those components are protectable. They should be considered the law firm's intellectual property. If a video recording of the presentation has been made, this is a third layer that can be protected.

An associate may also appear on a media outlet such as a local television station. Attorneys are often asked to provide broad legal perspective on a news story. While nothing the attorney says to the media may be covered by attorney-client privilege, the attorney's comments are captured by the third party and become content that is covered by the copyright of the third party.

In a situation such as this, where an attorney is interviewed by a media outlet, and wishes to publish this video on the firm's web site, appropriate permissions will need to be sought. In many instances, the attorney is best served addressing this issue prior to granting an interview.

Another external intellectual property issue may surface when a firm interacts with other law firms in a potentially of counsel or a contract scenario.

As an example, if one firm doesn't handle patent law, and it would like to contract with another firm to address a specific patent matter for its current client, the contract should be scrutinized to insure adequate protection for intellectual property issues. There can often be situations where information on one firm's process is exposed to the other firm.

An internal document that is shared, which may be as simple as an invoice, could reveal a specific method of doing business which may be considered an inadvertent revelation of a trade secret. Without appropriate precautions, that trade secret could become the property of the firm it has been shared with. The intellectual property rights and control of that creation could be lost. Protection against this type of loss can be provided within the contractual terms agreed to by the collaborating firms.

NOTES

Chapter 5

PROTECTING ARTISTIC CREATIONS BORN IN A LAW FIRM

❖ ❖ ❖

PUTTING COPYRIGHT NOTICE ON WORKS

One of the simplest ways to protect copyright is to insert the © symbol, the word "copyright," or the abbreviation "Copr."

It is also helpful to include the year of first publication of the copyrighted work along with the identification of the owner of the copyright.

This seems elementary. But for a law firm, any product that is drafted by an attorney, paralegal, admin, or a managing partner, most certainly a managing partner, should be produced in a templated structure. This can be in the form of either an electronic or physical document with the firm's letterhead. In either the header or footer the document clearly states...

- The law firm's proper and complete name
- The word "copyright"
- The year that the content was performed, written, and if appropriate, transcribed
- The © symbol for copyright

These four elements represent a notice to whomever comes across the creative work, whether in the form of a Word document, template, Power Point presentation, or some other representation, that this is content the author or authors are looking to protect.

More often than not, the firm's documents, templates, and even presentations, are reused.

It is important, especially when this content is presented to the public, that every single page contains the copyright information. This represents, without question, an affirmation that the rights created under that creative work do belong to the law firm, and also to the author or creator.

In the absence of this protection, the opposite holds true. When no notice is given to the public, the public may be in a rightful position to assume the content is either borrowed, or lacks a claim to rights.

Beyond the markings at the top or the bottom, traditionally at the bottom of the document, there may also be a registered trademark symbol (®) which provides notice that the preceding content is a trademark or service mark that has been registered.

As the years to go by, it is a good practice to review documents to insure proper protection. The "year" field for content creation may be auto populated. If it's not, there should be a manual process to review and update all documents to reflect the actual year of present day whenever an edit was made. This update is typically sufficient to address minor changes. More substantial changes that may affect the look, feel or content, should be covered in the copyright notice.

❖   ❖   ❖

THE COPYRIGHT REGISTRATION OF LEGAL CREATIONS

The process of protecting, and attempting to capitalize and package these creations within a law firm, or creations developed in the business of conducting a legal practice, is very much the same.

The process takes place through The Library of Congress, also known as the United States Copyright Office. The method is identical to any other creation, such as a solo artist or a business engaged in the creative works industry applies to protect.

That process begins with an application for registration at the Library of Congress, and it can cover different types of works:

- Audio
- Visual
- Written
- Sculptural
- Technical drawings
- 2D drawings
- Pictures
- Images
- Photographs

These can all be protected much like any other artist protects their creative works. The act of registering means the public is put on notice that the artist or the business that owns the art, in this case the law firm, intends on not only putting the public on notice, but has the intent of commercializing the creative works.

The reason for registering is what may be referred to as a "belt and suspenders" approach. As we've previously noted, the copyright protection, the copyright right as it were, is generated and created immediately upon fixing that creative expression to tangible means.

Simply because it is created at a given time doesn't mean anyone has been put on notice. In the event of legal proceeding stemming from an alleged violation, a court, judge, and jury would need to be provided with sufficient evidence to substantiate the fact that the author did indeed create the work on a specified date.

By registering the work with the Library of Congress, the copyright office acknowledges this claim to a creation date. It certifies the author, the title, and what the actual work is.

It captures a specimen of the work, usually through virtual means, such as a photograph or an electronic form of written description, or a reproduction of the work. This process captures exactly what was submitted so there is no question about who created the expression, what that expression entails, and the date on which it was created. This is the substantive information a judge requires to consider before making a ruling favorable to the infringed upon party.

There are two primary benefits to this process.

- To put the public at large on notice that you or your business intends to publish and/or commercialize one or more creative expressions, and by doing so will register the work and claim appropriate rights of ownership. This safeguards the content from usage without permission.

- To assure that if ever the copyrighted work needs to be enforced on an infringing party, that record is held and certified so that a judge or jury would not need to re-certify it. They would simply take the record as filed. At this point, the burden remains on the plaintiff to prove infringement. But the record and the actual body of the substance of the work would not be in question. This makes it easier for the plaintiff to enforce their copyrights.

❖ ❖ ❖

THE NEED FOR IP LAW FIRM COUNSEL

As law firms begin collecting intellectual property and identifying what warrants protection, time becomes a consideration.

For the firm that is not well versed in the processes and nuances of IP, it may be beneficial to seek counsel from a firm with a deeper grasp of these legal issues.

My firm, Bold IP, can be a valuable resource. We focus on intellectual property law, including patent prosecution & litigation, IP licensing, trademarks, copyright, and trade secrets.

Our work protecting IP with start-ups and emerging businesses means we are positioned to help leverage your firm's intellectual property assets and turn them into bottom-line profits.

Please call us at 1-206-899-0871 to schedule a no-obligation call. You can also schedule a consultation at:

http://www.boldip.com/bold-ip

Whatever direction you pursue, because of the information in this book, your firm now understands the basics of protection.

❖   ❖   ❖

ENGAGING THE IP FIRM

The firm you work with should be non-competitive.

For example, a family law firm would likely have no competitive issues with an IP firm, or any basis for ethical conflict.

Due diligence is advisable. Make sure the IP firm has a background of helping other law firms. Right now, this area of protection is something of a niche. Awareness of the issue is generally low, and while many of the basic legal approaches to protecting the firm's IP mirror those of protecting the assets of an engineering or technology company, there are some critical distinctions.

Seek out a firm that can demonstrate not only experience, but evidence of success. Time spent in the procedural mire and the muck may not prove sufficient. The work needs to be of high quality and needs to yield the results that your firm requires.

One request to make of any intellectual property law firm is to see evidence of their published and successful records. These can cover patent, copyright, trademark, or successful trade secret litigation settlements that are public record.

Keep in mind that much of what the firm does is not public. But there may be ample material that the firm can share with you. There may be additional disclosures the firm is not ethically obliged to provide. If they do share certain non-published information, this may constitute a breach of attorney-client privilege, a signal that this is a firm you most likely do not want to be working with.

An additional consideration involves the mechanics of the working relationship. The intellectual property law firm that works with another law firm should deliver services that are one-on-one, attorney to law firm.

There should not be layers of management or paralegals. Because so much can change both within the law firm and externally in the competitive environment, the relationship should be direct. This streamlines the process and helps to avoid possible conflicts.

NOTES

Chapter 6

SECRETS OF A LAW FIRM

❖ ❖ ❖

SECRETS, SYSTEMS, AND PROCESSES

It's important for the law firm to put structure, rules, and systems in place that attorneys, administrators, and paralegals can follow.

Many of these are designed and enhanced over time, which means we are dealing with a living document. This underscores the fact that in their current state, and at any given point in time, these processes and systems are highly valuable. They should be considered as trade secrets for law firms. Because of the nature of legal work, the processes employed by law firms often take on greater significance than those that might exist in another business.

Law firms must manage internal systems, determine how people communicate, and how documents are distributed and shared. But alongside internal systems are external processes. The firm is responsible for the clients' interests, which is paramount. From both ethical and business perspectives, it makes sense to be mindful that the responsibility of the firm to the client, and the ramifications of the work being done on the clients' behalf, can easily go well beyond that of a traditional business relationship.

The depth and substance of the relationship between the client and the firm justify designating systems and processes as trade secrets. The firm's unique approach to this must be protected.

All processes and systems must be documented. There should be digital records of the firm's systems, processes, and policies.

This is the heart of the matter. This procedure lies at the core of the firm, and it represents the work and vision of the firm's founders. This work allows the firm to distinguish itself and to move forward. These are truly the secrets of a law firm, bona fide trade secrets, and they should be protected against release so that their value is not surrendered and their trade secret status is not jeopardized.

When the actual documentation is performed, such as by saving a Microsoft Word document, the document should be clearly labeled and identified as a trade secret, or proprietary and for the law firm's internal use. The law firm's name should appear in the top, bottom, and within the header of document.

It should also be prominently displayed in training materials which provide access to systems and processes. This should cover situations such as:

- Onboarding
- When an employee is moving to a new role
- When other personnel move to a new role
- When retraining takes place

In these scenarios, communication should be distributed that informs participants of the proprietary nature of systems and process, and their unique attributes.

This constitutes trade secret information. It reflects:

- The way in which the firm conducts its business
- How the law firm competes
- How internal communication is managed
- How rules are set in place
- What events trigger activities inbound or outbound involving third parties or vendors
- How financial activities are determined and analyzed

Each one of these elements constitutes an underpinning of the firm's existence, what keeps it operational, profitable, and able to serve clients at a certain level of quality.

The architecture of how policies, systems, and processes are documented is somewhat arbitrary. In most instances, the more organized the information, the more valuable. The more formalized the structure, the greater degree of protection can be secured.

The trade secret is best protected when it is not a set of loose documents, but part of an organized structure, with a numbered process and system that could be duplicated.

In terms of the enforcement of this type of trade secret, a market value should be determined. Considerations for determining market value may include asking and answering questions such as:

"If an organized set of systems and processes turned up in the lap of a competing law firm, could this information be used immediately for economic gain?"

"Could a new law firm take this organized set of systems and processes, implement them, and begin to make money?"

The more likely scenarios such as these become, the higher the financial value the trade secret justifies.

The greater the number of potential barriers and re-strictions to access, the better. Each represents a dem-onstrated precaution to safeguard the trade secret status, so information remains intact, and the firm continues to prosper.

❖ ❖ ❖

THE PRICING ELEMENTS OF TRADE SECRETS

A critical aspect of trade secrets within a law firm revolves around pricing: pricing models, strategies, and approaches that determine how to frame different types of representation agreements with a client.

Firms often use different strategies for remuneration for their legal services. The processes and systems, the quoting mechanisms, or even the accounts receivable procedures are part of this. Collectively, they determine how the firm and the client interact financially.

Because this pricing strategy is unique to each firm, it should be considered a trade secret. This includes both the general practice pricing policies and the pricing itself, the actual numbers, the specific fees. The cost of the services should be considered a trade secret as well.

When a law firm uses a price sheet, or an hourly billing rate for their various associates, junior partners, partners, and managing partners, this is important and warrants protection. A key consideration involves the publishing of the fees. There may be situations where fee structures are not published so that pricing flexibility can be provided, and extenuating circumstances addressed.

The law firm should approach this by making sure employees understand pricing options that can be presented, and under which circumstances. Employees should understand the nature of confidentialities involved.

The firm may say, "We can perform services A, B, and C. We offer A to a particular client, but we have the ability to do B, C, and D. Fees for services B, C, and D are not typically communicated to the public." The employee is instructed that services B, C, and D represent options the firm makes available to select clients deemed appropriate under certain qualification strategies.

As an example, a client approaches the law firm of Bob Smith. Following an initial consultation, let's say the law offices of Bob Smith decides to engage and offer an engagement letter to take on a contractual matter.

The services are priced as a flat fee for a specific contract. Let's say the fee is presented as $1,000. The client responds by saying, "I can get this done elsewhere. I think I might be able to write it myself. That price just seems so high. Even after hearing about what you'll do, I think I'm going to have to look somewhere else."

The firm may now present options B, C, and D. Some of the options may be a payment plan structure where the law firm says, "We'd like to earn your business and bring you in. We understand that $1,000 may be a lot of money up front for you, so we'd like to be able to break up the payment. If you come up with $500 down, and then make payments, say $250 for the next two months to get to the even $1,000, we'd be fine doing that. We could also look at something more flexible, perhaps over the next 10 months, pay us $100 a month."

Some law firms are willing to take on work on a contingency basis. They will say, "I understand fees are hard to come by right now for you, but we're willing to take an ownership interest in either the business, the technology, or the patent as the legal work moves forward, and the royalties and the sales that come along with it."

(There are ethical issues to address with this type of a contingency fee, and while they aren't to be overlooked, they are not the focus of this book.)

The firm's pricing strategies may also include the option to simply defer payment altogether. It may say, "We love your idea. We love doing business with you. We want to help you with this contract. We're willing to provide services based on the understanding you will compensate us within 12 months."

The processes and systems that law firms design, provide, and execute to accomplish these types of payment terms are trade secrets. They should be considered part of the firm's suite of intellectual property.

❖   ❖   ❖

SECRETS LEAVING ATTORNEYS

Law firms, like many professionals, regularly collaborate.

When a law firm hires a junior associate, or when a junior level partner achieves a new partner level, each move represents different characteristics about the professional. These include the individual's skills, talents, and knowledge. This takes place both when someone new comes to the firm or is elevated to a higher level of responsibility.

We should keep in mind that there is always an option for that attorney to leave the firm. They may join the ranks of the solo practitioners and head off on their own.

Attorneys enjoy significant freedom, independence, willingness, and the ability to open up shop immediately. They do no need to seek employment elsewhere through an existing competitive firm. When they leave their firm to hang out their own shingle, they may potentially take clients from the previous firm with them.

In this type of scenario, the intellectual property covering the trade secrets and the internal knowledge of the firm becomes critical. The firm needs to protect itself and the employment contract in the sense that any of the trade secrets that are in the firm, to whatever degree possible, stay within the firm should attorneys depart.

In many instances, processes, systems, institutional knowledge and perhaps legal education and training is put to commercial use by attorneys that leave the firm.

One possible avenue to help mitigate the downsides of this is for the firm to launch a franchise type option.

The law firm could have an arm where the single attorney, if they wanted more independence, would be able to operate under the firm's name but enjoy more autonomy.

This autonomy would not be complete autonomy in a franchise model, given that the brands, the trademark, the logo, the image, the goodwill of the law firm are made available to an attorney or even a group of attorneys through intellectual property licensing agreements for a set period of time.

This type of structure allows the individual attorney to run their own practice, and maintain some of that trademark, goodwill, brand recognition that they and others at the firm have built up over the years.

In structuring this type of licensing arrangement, the firm should consider the different ways its brand could be leveraged. While the actual practice, and perhaps its clientele may enjoy autonomy, the overall image of the firm presented to the public remains congruent with the brand attributes of the original firm.

To insure proper protection for the law firm's interest, guidelines should be developed to cover exactly how the attorney will be using the name. Any limitations or restrictions on acceptable usage should be covered in detail in the licensing agreement.

❖ ❖ ❖

PROTECTING THE FIRM'S CLIENT INFORMATION

The client list represents one of the law firm's most closely guarded and highly valued trade secrets. This list keeps the business moving. The firm should keep this client list readily available but appropriately protected for internal access, and it should be organized.

Under ethical rules and guidelines, to maintain the confidentiality of client information, the electronic or physical storage of client files should be secure and encrypted. When the client list is digitally maintained, all files should be secure, not only with ample password protection, but through encryption. Encryption should be sufficiently strong that in the event a third party were to gain access, it would be unable to read the files, collect the information, and put it to use.

Client files should be organized and displayed in a manner that makes the information readily prepared for other attorneys to perform conflict checking.

Along with the nuances of properly organizing and maintaining client files, the actual client information constitutes a trade secret. This information includes:

- The list of individual people
- The people within the business that is a firm's businesses client
- Contact information including address, phone number and email
- Notes and the file history

This information, or parts of it, which is housed and protected within the firm, may need to be exchanged with a third party. This happens in scenarios where a counsel attorney or a co-counsel situation arises where a law firm or a solo practitioner needs to share client information. Information is shared with a third-party attorney, or perhaps a non-attorney, to conduct business and move the client's interests forward.

In all cases, the client should acknowledge the need to share relevant information and provide express permission to do so.

The trade secret belongs to the law firm as far as the client information is concerned. In an exchange with a potential of counsel, at a minimum, a non-disclosure agreement is required. This is a bilateral agreement where the law firm agrees to learn about potential conflicts of the oncoming attorney of counsel to determine if conflicts exist.

The potential of counsel attorney agrees to not disclose, misappropriate, or use inappropriately, either the client information the trade secret information from the law firm that they may potentially perform services for.

A similar situation arises with a co-council situation where an entire firm is being brought on. The firm may perform specialized aspects of litigation assistance, to provide discovery, or some other aspect of the representation. There will be a need to exchange client information.

The two law firms, in collaboration, should use a bilateral non-disclosure agreement that insures all necessary agreements are in place, and are enforceable in the state or states where the two parties are contracting.

Situations may arise where a client moves from one law firm to another. The actual transfer process of the file should be addressed thoroughly. Client histories need to be maintained so that that they can be shipped or securely transferred.

NOTES

Chapter 7

PROTECTING THE TRADE SECRETS OF THE LAW FIRM

Trade secrets are most effectively protected by making sure that they are enforceable. If a third-party were to misappropriate or steal a trade secret, a law firm would need to show the court that it had taken all the necessary steps to safeguard its improperly used content.

❖ ❖ ❖

SUCCESSFULLY ESTABLISHING INDEPENDENT ECONOMIC VALUE

- The firm should establish the existence of independent economic value through its ability to monetize the content.

- Both the process of monetizing the content, which could range from an internal procedural document to an external marketing presentation, may be considered trade secrets with independent economic value.

❖ ❖ ❖

DEMONSTRATING REASONABLE PROTECTIVE PRECAUTIONS

- The firm must show that it has made sufficient efforts to keep the content secure, and that the underlying subject matter of the trade secret is indeed proprietary.
- It needs to be demonstrated that the content in question is not readily ascertainable by the public. The information is not something that the public could easily find online, published in a newspaper, or accessed from the third-party's own knowledge about the industry.
- It should be shown that the information in question has either been calculated or has been gathered over time, through experience or through knowledge that is accrued by doing the work of the law firm.

❖ ❖ ❖

DEMONSTRATING IMMEDIATE ECONOMIC VALUE TO A COMPETITOR

- It must be independently verified and established by a third-party, or proven in court by the litigant, that the content provides independent economic value to a competitor.
- This economic value means the third-party can monetize this content, either immediately, over time, or both.
- A classic trade secret within a law firm is a client list with names, addresses, and contact information. This list should be labeled as a trade secret.
- The content in question is clearly designated as protected through the use of specific words such as "confidential" and "proprietary."
- The firm can show that access is limited. If encryption has been used, this protective effort is shown as an active step taken to protect a trade secret.

NOTES

Chapter 8

✢ ✢ ✢

INVENTING IN THE LAW FIRM

The nature of the firm is to refine, improve, and enhance. This can easily lead to a variety of inventions, which may qualify for protection.

❖　❖　❖

CO-INVENTOR ATTORNEYS

As an advisor and a counselor to different businesses and individuals, a law firm, especially an intellectual property law firm, may work with inventors. Over the course of this work the firm may become part of the invention process.

There are situations where law firms can be considered inventors. The attorneys which make up the firm can be named as co-inventors if they contribute to the creation of the intellectual property surrounding a patent.

It is not unusual for a situation to arise where an attorney with an intellectual property law firm works with a client, and after discussing an invention with the client, suggests one or more embodiments, versions, or applications of the invention the client did not consider.

This may involve different types of technology, such as implementations with computers or software. Based on the firm's agreement with the client, it may be entitled to an assignment privilege and possible ownership of any rights of a co-inventor.

❖ ❖ ❖

HIGH LEVEL PATENTS SOFTWARE

Over the course of a firm's ongoing work, attorneys, paralegals, and other staff members may generate patentable subject matter. This can result from people who apply their knowledge and develop processes on the conduct of business that deal with clients and other attorneys. This subject matter may cover:

- Certain nuances and approaches a legal analysis may involve

- The optimum information flows for the collection of information
- The actual generation of transactional documents

Over time, processes such as these may be improved far beyond the original approach. The procedures may be refined well beyond what is typical in the traditional landscape of the practice area. In the context of software and its application, factors include:

- How research is conducted
- How documents are generated
- How words are typed
- How lawyers communicate with other lawyers
- How lawyers communicate with other clients

What this signifies is the creation of a unique and utilitarian expression. It represents a novel and non-obvious function.

Software is widely used for managing information flows, data transmittal, and information about the client or other attorneys. It can embrace communication, storage, redistribution, and automation.

The distinctive aspects of automation provided by software can represent a particularly valuable area to protect. The firm may be using an in-house software platform to streamline the process of publishing on social media platforms, or a similar application that supports the firm's marketing functions.

❖   ❖   ❖

MARKETING

Like any other business, law firms are now competing in an increasingly complex marketing environment. They need to showcase their area of skill and expertise in one or more practice areas. Through these marketing channels they acquire clients and grow their business. Because law firms are now more proactive in their marketing, they use systems to manage the different processes of marketing, such as lead acquisition and the conversion of prospective clients to actual clients.

This process is largely predicated on a classic sales process. In many ways, it is similar to what we see with other traditional business, although the law firm is bound by more stringent regulations. There are also considerations of security and privacy that may impact the process of marketing, which could extend to the underlying attorney-client privilege.

Aside from regulatory, privacy, and security issues germane to all law firms, the sales process and the sales cycle it creates, can be built around unique attributes. These may involve a process the firm follows to identify target clients in a specific manner, how best to approach them, and the most effective ways to qualify them as prospective clients.

These sort of sub-processes, as long as they generate novel functions, automation, or some type of utility, may represent intellectual property that can be patentable or otherwise protected. The litmus test involves differentiating these sub-processes from what currently exists, and what has been developed in the past.

NOTES

Chapter 9

❖ ❖ ❖

PROTECTING INVENTIONS IN THE LAW FIRM

❖ ❖ ❖

PATENTING BASICS

Protecting inventions in a law firm, once they have been created, and based on the fact the attorney has taken a role as an inventor or a co-inventor, is very much the same as with any other invention.

The first step involves an understanding of patent eligibility.

Surprisingly, most inventions are patent eligible. We are generally dealing with inventions, typically some type of utility invention and utility patent application as opposed to design. There are different criteria for each, and a distinction is drawn between utility and design.

Utility inventions perform functions. They tend to be mechanical, electrical, and chemical. They provide a novel and non-obvious result that has never been seen before.

The threshold question is eligibility. A few years ago, software patenting issues came under fire by the United States Supreme Court. On June 19, 2014, the Court ruled in Alice Corp. v. CLS Bank International that "merely requiring generic computer implementation fails to transform [an] abstract idea into a patent-eligible invention."

This ruling should prompt us to consider whether the invention itself, especially if it involves software, is more akin to what the courts have ruled as abstract subject matter and akin to natural laws.

Mathematical algorithms, mathematical formulae involve natural laws.

Even if a mathematician solved a new equation, the fact that we are dealing with an equation means we are proving what already exists in nature, and this is not patentable. It is a law of nature. The work done to create a solution is significant, but it may not be controlled by one or more individuals. It is part of the public domain.

Abstract ideas fall into a similar vein. Concepts that cannot be affixed to a tangible or physical world, or attached to any other actual and demonstrable change, in either material or electronic nature, are not patentable.

This is what the United States Supreme Court ruled on in Alice Corp. v. CLS Bank International.

In this case, the patent that was being accused of being invalid dealt with a particular business method. It involved the connection between one computer database and another, where the interface would result in information to make automatic decisions on financial markets and exchange rates.

The Supreme Court ruled that because the work of that invention takes place without any human interaction, and without the ability to see or even react to what has taken place, that no visible or actual change takes place between the databases.

The court ruled that the invention was too abstract to warrant protection and that it invalidated a patent already in force, which was held by CLS Bank.

The laws have evolved somewhat and criteria has changed. But the eligibility question and considerations of abstraction should be evaluated early in the process of securing legal protection for an invention.

Assuming that the invention is eligible under patent law, Section 101 of Title 35 of the United States Code, the next consideration involves actual patentability. Patentability is generally determined by two factors.

The first is novelty and a determination if something is new. It should be determined what else currently exists and how new it is. If there is an improvement, the depth and significance of these benefits and enhancements need to be identified and substantiated.

The second factor considers whether the invention is non-obvious to someone in the field of innovation.

Patentability analysis should be performed before a formal patent application is drafted. A professional patent attorney or patent agent can work on this type of a search.

The inventor should have a grasp of both business and technical issues, so that when the time comes to draft the application, there are no questions concerning the novel aspects of the invention.

Generally, there will be a patent awarded when those two hurdles are cleared. The question then becomes to what degree and what type of rights will the inventor have?

❖   ❖   ❖

ENFORCING AND PROTECTING

Like all inventions and creations registered with the USPTO as patents or patent publications, once submitted these assets can be protected through different means of monitoring.

A law firm can retain an intellectual property law firm to monitor the competitive landscape, proactively seek out instances of infringement, and insure that their rights are being enforced. This process can begin once a patent is granted. The IP firm can perform due diligence, either on a weekly or monthly basis depending on the nature of the industry and its rate of change.

What about the situation where possible infringement has been identified?

There may be a competitor which is not aware of the fact another firm has already secured a patent, and is making, using, selling, or importing goods or services within the United States where the law firm has rights.

When this happens, the infringed upon firm has different options. One could be writing a cease and desist letter, a process covered in Chapter 3. This letter would prevent the other party from taking any action in the marketplace, and would put the party on notice of the infringement offense.

At this point, we typically see negotiations occur. Depending on how invested the infringing party is, we could see a licensing agreement where the new market entrant is obligated to pay a royalty to the law firm which holds patents and protection over its creations.

There are other ways to acquire patent rights for a law firm. One is through a fee agreement with the inventor. Within the provisions there may be an agreement that if payments are not made by the inventor to the firm, the invention rights are assigned to the firm. In this case, the law firm then becomes the owner of the intellectual property because the client failed to abide by terms of the agreement.

In a situation such as this, where the creation was not born in the firm itself, it is not owned by the firm. Protecting that asset becomes a top priority, as does leveraging the asset and making sure it is used to its greatest benefit. Either through the work of its own attorneys, or by retaining an intellectual property litigation firm, those rights can be enforced.

Those rights can also be proactively brokered. Licensees and buyers can be sought to acquire the asset in question. There are companies that focus purely on patent brokering, and a vibrant market exists with buyers and sellers.

This market may prove profitable for the law firm that has secured proper protections for its IP, and has rights to a product or products for which there is demand. This can easily provide a new revenue stream for the firm and allow it to enjoy the leverage that comes with additional assets on its books.

NOTES

Chapter 10

CONCLUSION

As you have now discovered, the entire process of identifying IP, safeguarding it and monetizing it, is largely predicated on common sense.

The law firm should begin by remembering it performs as a business. It should keep in mind that over time, what may seem like small and incremental improvements to its systems and processes add up. The result can easily be something that is unique and utilitarian that qualifies for protection.

Simple documentation goes a long way to securing the level of protection that allows the firm to create profitable IP assets.

It has been my pleasure to share this information with you. Hopefully, you will start to take the simple steps to identify your intellectual property and take a fresh look at the types of creations you can safeguard.

You have an opportunity to better define the benefits of your firm to the public, to help prospective clients better understand and appreciate your capabilities, and value the quality of your work.

Intellectual property plays a vital role in this.

To support you with this initiative, we are providing a checklist, a framework for an audit, so you can simplify the process and take meaningful steps forward.

NOTES

The Law Firm's Intellectual Property Audit

❖ ❖ ❖

Identification Of Areas Of IP Protection

- ✓ Computer science applications and processes have been identified
- ✓ Software developments for the firm's management have been identified
- ✓ Software developments for the firm's client relationship management have been identified
- ✓ Novel methods for marketing have been identified
- ✓ Innovative processes for handling clients have been identified

✓ The firm's brand has been defined and appropriate distinctions have been identified

✓ Protections are considered not only for the present, but for the long-term, and should prepare for possible mergers, acquisitions, and other changes in the firm's structure

❖ ❖ ❖

THE PROACTIVE PROCESS OF SAFEGUARDING DOMESTICALLY

✓ Applications have been submitted to the USPTO trademark office

✓ These applications cover elements of the firm's brand such as a logo and a name

✓ Separate applications have been submitted to protect internal documents, processes, and systems

✓ Copyright notice has been placed on all appropriate works

❖ ❖ ❖

THE PROACTIVE PROCESS OF SAFEGUARDING GLOBALLY

- ✓ Applications made to the USPTO have also been submitted to either the World Intellectual Property Organization or through the Madrid Protocol

❖ ❖ ❖

ENFORCEMENT MEASURES

- ✓ The framework of a cease and desist letter has been prepared to use in instances of possible infringement
- ✓ A firm has been retained to monitor the marketplace for possible instances of infringement

❖ ❖ ❖

OTHER

- ✓ Proper protections are put in place for the firm's IP prior to collaboration with another firm on behalf of a client
- ✓ When work is created through collaboration with another firm, appropriate protections are secured
- ✓ As IP issues are identified, the benefits of retaining an outside IP firm are weighed